Chaundra is a very hard-working dedicated worker she is well grounded, educated, family oriented and a very happy motivated woman when she puts her mind to accomplishing a task she sees it through to the end ,she is not a quitter but most of all just an overall truly great person to know, to know her is to love her she is very inspirational and believes in God, she fights for her country and her family structure, she's a winner !!!

-Rentha Blandin

Chaundra is one of my dearest friends. We've known each other for about 17 years and she's always been outgoing with a positive personality. A wonderful Mother and Wife. Sometimes we have to encourage ourselves but it's always great when you have a friend like Chaundra to help you along the way.

— Sherell Thomas

Let me start by saying Chaundra Gore is a true prayer warrior. She is that person that will not judge you not matter what. You can go to her with a problem and immediately she will ask if she can pray with you. Her love is genuine, and you can see compassion in every aspect of her being. Chaundra has done nothing but shown me the calling that God has on her life from the day that I met her, and she is destined to fulfill that calling. She is a strong follower of Christ and she is an avid business woman. She is purpose driven and very intentional. A mighty Woman of God!

— Traci McDowell

There are not enough words to say about this phenomenal woman, who not only inspires others daily but is a true light for others. Since the first day I met my Soror and now my Sister of which blood connection could not have done any better I knew I had met someone special. This sister has been down a path that no one could understand and has come on top. Her true and strong faith in God is what guides her daily, her love of her family is bar none. The sacrifices that she makes for them and her eye on a better future inspires others *to Level Up and stand up. An ultimate woman serving in the military that has guided so many service members to do better. Who else can inspire you but Chaundra Gore "LensofFaith Speaks"!!!! I can't wait!!*

- Michelle Radix

Mrs. Gore is so sweet spirited. The first time that we encountered one another she has always brighten up the room. I look forward to the encouragement and spiritual presence that she brings. Mrs. Gore keep doing what you do because there's a message for everyone.

— Pamela Wesley

You are such a blessing! God has truly done a great work and will continue to do a great work in you. I cannot wait to see where you go from here!

— Diane Adams, Maximum Transformations, LLC

I've known Chaundra for over 20 years and the transformation from then to now is amazing. She is a beautiful person, a loving and dedicated wife and mother. Chaundra is a God-fearing woman of integrity and she is passionate about her job, business, family, and friends. Chaundra is a compassionate person and she speaks so eloquently about the people and things she loves.

-Monica Thomas

Chaundra is one of the most charismatic, energetic, cheerful and strong-minded persons I know. Her leadership traits are quite encouraging and motivating. She is a strong advocate of "can do attitude". A true pleasure to have as friend and as a battle buddy.

– Rico Cruz, Sergeant First Class, U.S. Army (Retired)

Mrs. Gore, when I first meet her, we click. She like my mentor and she don't even know it when I need someone to talk to I can always call her. She one of the ladies I look up too. Amazing powerful women I've meet in 2 years.

— Nagee Merriman

Chaundra is Amazing. She is passionate, attentive, loving, and humble. Chaundra is one to emulate. She gives realistic advice and she's very supportive. Not only does she talk the talk, but she walks the walk. Thank you Chaundra for your positive attitude and prayers. Love you

- Moneka Smith, Founder of Kappa Epsilon Psi Military Sorority, Inc.

Chaundra Gore is awesome!! I've known her for 18 years. She was one of my Army basic training Soldiers. Even then, as a teenager, I could see the leadership ability that she possessed. She was a leader by her actions, the example she set, and vocally...even motivating the troops on her platoon and company back then!! Recently I had the honor to hear her radio interview and I was blown away by it. I'm not easily impressed but she knocked my socks off in that interview. I was motivated by her and ready to run through a wall! I know things haven't been easy for her and she has had more than her share of trials and tribulations. Unlike some, she used her trials as a means to learn and grow to become a better person. She didn't use excuses or let it hamper her. She is an amazing woman and a phenomenal speaker. I haven't been that captivated by words and a true testimony in years. I'm honored to call her a friend and a great motivational speaker! I could go on forever about her, but I will stop here. Thank you for the opportunity to sing her praises as a person and motivational speaker. Awesomeness at its best...Chaundra Gore!!

-Derrick Maffett, Command Sergeant Major, U.S. Army (Retired)

My mother is an inspiration to me and hope to many others out there. Since my mother has started her journey of speaking out about what she truly believes in is just amazing to me. When she first started doing her photography, she didn't just want to do photography, she wanted to tell a story through her pictures. My mother is a WOMAN OF SUBSTANCE, and she wants other women to feel that they are as well. My mother as supported in everything that I do, and she really pushed me and my other siblings to do great. Me and my siblings may think she's being mean, but she just truly wants us to excel to our fullest ability and more. When I heard my mother on a podcast, she did it brought tears to my eyes because I knew that she was a powerful woman, mother, wife, daughter, leader and much more when she spoke the words she spoke. Now my mother is excelling abundantly with her business and her new book she is in the making of with fellow women of substance. Lastly to say, I am truly honored to be the daughter of Chaundra Gore.

-(My Daughter – Makiyah Isles)

Chaundra is powerful! Her words are lifting and encouraging. She gives you the feeling that possibility are limitless when you operate in your purpose. Great spirit and radiant energy that will set your heart on fire.

— LaShonda H. Henderson, LMHC

Truly uplifting and Amazing! Her words provide spiritual guidance. relief and hope. She provides you the strengthen to walk into your purpose and do great things just by speaking the truth and having Faith. She has been a Blessing to me from the first day we met, and I am beyond grateful to have her in my life!

-Natasha Fogerty, Service Coordinator, Veterans Affairs Wounded Warrior Program

From the first time we met, I knew that she was a very positive and uplifting type of person. She has been one of the few lasting, truthful and inspirational persons I have met throughout my life. Her words speak life into a situation that may seem impossible! Thanks for being who you are!!

-LaQuita Lawson, SSG, U.S. Army

CEO Gore is a powerhouse of inspiration and commitment. Since I have known her, there has been a since of structure over her life, in her ability to shine light into the lives of others. Her humbling experience and spirit gives comfort to continuing to find your purpose and living in it.

– Shannon M. Little, Founder Joyful Soul Treasures, Inc.

Mrs. Gore is an intelligent, kind-hearted, transparent, and God-fearing woman. She quickly disarms all she meets with her warm smile and uplifting dialogue. She is on the move delivering her message of how hope and investing in herself is opening up doors everywhere. Anyone who hears her story will be renewed!

- Tamiko Brown, U.S. Army (Retired) Veteran

How do you describe this great woman? Rooted in faith and love for family, friends and mankind. She makes everyone welcomed. She is a hard worker, a great wife and mother. Honored to know her.

- Kimberly Gore

An Ambitious, Phenomenal, Amazing woman who is an Inspiration to us all. She is a woman of solitude and grace. She will brighten up a room whenever she walks in. A woman of spiritual growth. A woman of substance!

- Michelle Williams

She never ceases to amaze me. The traveling back and forth and workload, yet family, friends, strangers and organizations all are presented with her at her best. Her dedication to doing the work required of her is phenomenal. She brings a wealth of fresh air to any room she enters. She is a Shining Light.

– Veronica Tal, VP Savannah River Chapter Federally Employed Women

At first you think, where did this woman get such a powerful voice, but then you realize she has always carried herself in a manner that commands respect. We love you Mrs. Gore and I quote from the late great Mr. Dennis Green formerly of the Minnesota Vikings: " She is whom, we thought she is"!!

- (My Husband Mr. Kenneth Gore)

I am proud to introduce Mrs. Chaundra Gore!! She is a purpose driven, energetic, exceptional woman of God who wears many hats and wears them radiantly! She's been through a lot, but always lets her light shine through adversity!! She is a true inspiration to all who encounter her warmth, kindness, leadership and sense of humor!!

-Samara Walker, U.S. Air Force Veteran

Chaundra Gore is an inspiration to all she meets. She consistently displays a positivity and has a clear vision. Her ability to not communicate effectively and overall personality draws you in. Being able to relate to her audience and even providing personal experiences is a quality that is invaluable. I can't wait to hear her speak again. Congratulations and keep it up. We need more positive, black, female women in this world.

- Ashley McGriff, SSG, U.S. Army

Your work with others is simply amazing. Thank you for sharing your time and encouraging words to uplift everyone. Keep doing what God has called you to do and watch your broadcast expand. This is wonderful! #Godsplan

- Ashley Flanigan-Lee

Phenomenal and inspirational person, and Soldier. I've had the privilege of listening to her speak and provide wisdom which carried me through my hard times of life. I highly recommend listening to her speeches and utilizing her photography services.

- Carlos Jones

Very passionate! Chaundra is one of the most supportive women I know of other women. It has been an absolute pleasure getting to know her & watching her excel leaps & bounds. She is definitely one you would want in your Network!

- Regina "MsGina" Cotton, I~Motivate Solutions, LLC

I am a LENS OF FAITH

I am a LENS OF FAITH

CHAUNDRA NICOLE GORE, MSL

I Am a Lens Of Faith

Copyright © 2019 by Chaundra Nicole Gore

All rights reserved

No part of this book may be used or reproduced in any manner whatsoever without written permission except in the case of brief quotations embodied in critical articles and reviews.

FIRST EDITION

Book design by Allison Arnett of www.branditbeautifully.com

ISBN 978-0-578-45612-6

Scriptures are from the King James Bible unless otherwise indicated.

Dedication

I dedicate this book to all the women who have suffered, cried, been broken, suffered abuse, anguish, abandonment, suicide, the loss of a child, sickness or disease, marriage trouble, career trials and many other tribulations. As long as you have breath in your body, you can change the way your story ends. Use Faith, prayer, and the power of God to turn your mess into a message for the women behind you. For, she needs to know just how YOU MADE IT THROUGH!

Table of Contents

ACKNOWLEDGEMENTS 1

FOREWORD 3

A LETTER TO MY CHILDREN 7

POWER 13

THE WAITING ROOM 27

I LOVE BEING A MOTHER 49

ADOPTED 69

FAITH FIGHT 75

THE UNITED STATES ARMY 81

MEDICAL DIAGNOSIS 87

REAR VIEW MIRROR 93

A LENS OF FAITH 99

ABOUT THE AUTHOR 103

Acknowledgements

First, giving honor to God who is the head of my life, without him this would not be possible. Thank you, God for giving me every trial and tribulation, that has allowed me to deliver this message of faith and encouragement.

I am forever grateful for my husband, mothers, children, nieces, sisters, cousins, and extended family that have supported me and gave me strength and encouragement at one time or another in person, via phone, or virtually through the good and the bad. I am also glad that God connected me to these power house women and men of God, that I have personally connected with to encourage me, listen to me, and support me along this journey called life: My mother Judy Wyndham, Kathy Smith, Pastor Jomo Cousins, Minister Valencia Wright, Pastor Marcus Wright, Prophetess Crystal Cunningham, Star Holmes-Word, Dr.

Ranelli Williams, Donna Hicks Izzard (The D.I.), Aprille Franks (Spark and Hustle Conference), Kim Jones, Marilyn Norris, Kimberly Gore, LaTanya Donald, Regina Cotton, Tomelya Coley, Diane Adams, Keywana Wright, Peggy Melendez, Geanice Barganier, Melissa Starks, and LaShonda Henderson.

Lastly, this book project would not have come together so effortlessly without an editor, formatter, cover designer, photographer, make artist and hair stylist. Thank you, Christian Cashelle, Allison Arnett, Megan Elise Photography, Morgan Starks, and Mercedes Mckinney. Everything worked together for the good. I appreciate each of you.

Foreword

What an honor it is to introduce the world to an amazing journey by such a faith filled woman. I met Chaundra in 1997 while in high school. Both of our parents were absent and through our friendship we supported each other. We did a lot together, from travelling to France on exchange, to getting our first jobs, cars, and stabilizing our lives together. Her journey is amazing, and I believe that sharing it will liberate others.

Chaundra has been through plenty of trials in her life. From gaining emancipation at 14, to running a household, to protecting/serving our country as a Soldier, to growing a healthy and worthy American family.

In my own journey, my mother moved away when I was 10 and my father, an alcoholic, kicked me out when I was fifteen because I reminded him and his girlfriend of my mother. They hated that I was willing to walk miles to church and left them little notes about the ills of drinking and smoking. At 15, Nicole and I knew our path.

My father kicking me out was the best thing that could ever happen to me. I got a job at Footlocker, maintained my honors record, and went off to an elite college. From there I completed Harvard and MIT, traveled the world and I'm now living my dreams.

In 2015, I founded my startup, EcoTech Visions, a company that is committed to creating jobs, sustaining community, and protecting the planet through growing communities of entrepreneurs. We started in Miami and are expanding throughout the Southeast and Midwestern USA. I have a great relationship with my parents as we are all in this life to live our own paths. Nicole and I knew our purpose earlier than most and have been walking alongside each other ever since. Success is not about your circumstances, but rather how you respond to them and what you chose to live for.

Chaundra is an inspiration to us all. Her grounding is her spiritual center. We all stumble but she is a shining example of what it means to feed one's soul with the image and likeness of God. Even with all of her various titles and responsibilities, Chaundra takes the time out of her daily walk to praise God and help others realize His strength through her testimony. Her persistence and faith in God's promises, will uplift and motivate you to push past your own ideals and thoughts to focus on God's vision for your life.

    I believe that *I Am a Lens of Faith* is going to heal, deliver, and set free this generation and those to come. You will find that your story may compare to hers, but she wants you to know that no matter what you go through in life, you can grow through it by keeping your faith in God.

Dr. Pandwe Gibson, Ph.D

CHAPTER ONE

A Letter to My Children

Life happens to everyone. The dash in between your birth date and the date you die should have meaning, purpose, and a legacy for your children. To my children, I love you with all my heart and I want you to know that everything I have gone through and grown from was destined to sow better seeds for you. I want you to exceed what I have done for you and do better for your children. I have taught you to be educated, strong, courageous, tough, resilient, effective, humble, kind, loving, and dedicated. Fight the good fight, finish the course, keep the faith, and God will carry you the rest of the way.

I want you to be leaders and not followers. Can you answer these questions? What do you want to be when you are all grown up? What legacy are you building for your family? What is your why? Establish your destiny, prepare your goals, work hard for what you want to achieve, and reach them. Focus your time on things above and not things below, the positive and not the negative. Follow only God's path for your life and not the way of the world. You have the power to lead and lead effectively. You have the talent to lead and take your business, talent, and skills to greater heights.

Never try to be someone else. Be the best version of you, the most authentic person you can be. Never allow temptation to capture your mind or allow it to cause you to think like someone else. Be you and love you. I know you can do or be anything you set your mind to. Make sure your word is your bond, mean what you say and say what you mean. Be confident in who you are and know whose you are. You are a child of the Most High God. Remember this: strength lies within, you don't need anyone to validate you. God gave you a promise, a gift, and a talent. It's up to you to discover it and exercise it!

Focus on setting the best example you can for your children. Life isn't easy. There will be some tough days, seasons, and trials and tribulations that you must lean on God to get through. *"Fear God and give Him all the glory, because the hour of judgment has come*, (Revelation 14:7)."

"God has not given me a spirit of fear, but of power, love and a sound mind, (2 Timothy 1:7)." Remember these words, my children. Get to know God personally and allow his hands to be placed upon you. It took me a long time to embrace who God wants me to be, but it is never too late to put God first. Don't get so caught up in the materialistic life that you forget whose you really are. God allowed you to be present on purpose, so find out what your God-given purpose is. Don't ever be afraid to step out front and be as bold as

a lion and take charge of your destiny. Destiny awaits us all and the sooner you can accept the real you, you will be just fine.

Malik, your name is Hebrew and it means KING, so you are already destined for greatness. Stand up tall, head up, chest out, and walk like the king you are. Embrace who you are and never be afraid to own who you are. Makiyah, your name is Hebrew, and it means who is like God. You are already destined for greatness. You have a huge heart for others, and you carry the weight of others. Embrace who God says you are and don't ever be afraid of failing because failure molds us into who we become for God. Chloe, your name is Greek, and it represents the fertility goddess, but it also means blooming. I know you sometimes struggle with self-esteem and you don't like to get things wrong. God made you to blossom right where you are, and you are doing just that. Always remember how long it takes a plant to grow and for its flowers to blossom. Kendrick, your name is Scottish/Welsh and it means greatest champion and family ruler. You have embraced the meaning of your name from the day you were born. You rule our house and boss everyone around in it. I told your dad that you have been here before. You take charge of everything and you are a true champion.

Watch out for the devil, he comes to steal, kill, and destroy your life. He never looks like who you think of in your mind. He comes in the form of friends, family, co-workers, social media, and emails. Be mindful of the relationships you establish. Ask yourself why that particular person is in your life and make sure it's for the right reason. You will make mistakes, but the key is to learn from your mistakes. God will make you repeat a season, if you don't grow from the season He put you in. Everything happens for a reason in a season.

In this life you will have tribulation, but be of good cheer. Nothing comes by surprise to God, but it will be a surprise to you. Fight with the sword of the spear, which is the word of God. Trust God's plan for your life and know that He is always with you no matter what. Anytime you face a hard situation, give it to God. The battle is not yours, it's the Lord's. God can handle things far better than we can, so give it all to Him. As your mother, I have fought all my fights in prayer after learning that the physical earthly battle was too hard, strenuous, stressful, and nerve wrecking. Now I fight in my war room, which is a room I designated to pray on my knees and display all that God has told me to bring to Him and leave with Him. Now you go and create your WAR ROOM.

I love you dearly.

Love always, Mom.

CHAPTER TWO

Power

How is it that when you plug your television up and press power, it turns on and displays your favorite show? How is it that you can put a battery in your car and the lights will turn on? How is it that you can go to church, listen to the word of God, and go home depressed? The only difference between the first two questions and the last question is that one uses electrical current and the other one takes initiative on your part to call out to God and tap into His power for your life. All He asks is for you to commit to Him and put nothing before Him. It took me a number of years to tap into the power God had for me. I knew God, but was estranged from Him because I wanted to do things my way. I wanted to date who I wanted to date, listen to what I wanted to listen to, and entertain the wrong people. As a matter of fact, I allowed a messy circle of negative people to engulf my life and mind with foolishness. I thought it was funny to be mean. As a teenager and young adult, I thought it was just to treat people exactly how they treated me. As I grew older, responsibility became very real to me and I discovered that I made every decision; good or bad.

For a while, I blamed my dad for all of my mistakes.

"If you didn't die, I would be well off and living good, Dad," I thought. "It's because you died that I am the way I am."

Well, as I look back over my life, I know God allowed me to go through that season so that I could testify about it right now. I neglected the power God had for me because I was walking in the flesh and doing whatever I wanted to do without asking God first. See, it's easy to place blame on others and forget to look in the mirror at yourself. I swear I've walked past the mirror, looked in it and never evaluated who I really was until I put God first in my life.

If we just take time to connect with God's power, He will walk with you, talk with you, and guide you every step of the way, according to His will and purpose for your life. God has taken me on a journey I will never forget and I have learned many lessons. I have now plugged my life into His hands and I am a force so powerful that the devil is confused. The devil has to get out of my way now because I am blessed and highly favored. Once I realized that, I gained the power to break barriers, destroy yokes, cut the snare of the enemy to pieces, drive the devil out, and live a healthier life. I can actually feel the connection I have with God. Once I plugged into God's power, I started to see things I never thought were possible for my life. God changed my circle, one person at a time. He replaced every bad relationship with professional, wealthy, strong, courageous, determined, happy, and encouraging men and women that have added to the good order and power for my life. God is at the top of it all. It was through Him that I became a woman of substance.

You have to use the power of the Lord to change your circumstance as I did for my marriage, my job, my career path, my children, and myself. I prayed like it was nobody's business for my son, whom they told me had a developmental delay because he was born premature. I took myself to the ER after developing chest pains while having a heated argument with the father of my son. My blood pressure was raised and I thought I was having a heart attack. I got to the hospital and it was bradycardia. I was told my baby would need to be delivered at 29 weeks. I couldn't believe what was happening. He is now a strong, young black boy that is currently a sophomore progressing successfully. He still has some struggles, but he has come a mighty long way by the grace of God. He struggled with reading comprehension and being organized all through elementary school. As a 9th grader, we discovered he was an audible learner and reads best by listening to the audiobook version as he follows along. It may have taken us 15 years to figure that out, but better now than never. I tried several things at each school he attended and he has been progressing quite well. I was told he would be dyslexic and struggle with speech, but God has been walking with my son every step of the way.

    I discovered my oldest daughter had a heart condition called ventricular tachycardia, but God healed her after a 7-year battle to repair her heart. You may not know what it feels like to take your 3-year-old to the hospital for a fever and then being medically evacuated to a children's hospital because her heart was beating too fast at rest. All I heard was, "Stat," and the monitor beeping as if it flatlined. She was still sitting and waiting on the doctor to return. I had no idea everyone was rushing to her room because something was wrong. I thought the machine was just malfunctioning because my baby looked fine, she just had a fever. I got on my knees and prayed for her day in and day out, every hour, every doctor's visit, every time it crossed my mind. Seven years later, she had a repeat oblation done and it fixed her heart. She has a big heart with a lot of love. If you ever get the chance to meet her, you will see how amazing she really is. I know God smiled on her and she is living her life as a young teenage entrepreneur.

My baby girl was born with what the doctors called tyrosinemia which is a liver condition. I prayed from the day they diagnosed her until God said there is nothing wrong. It was our prayers as husband and wife that moved that mountain called disease from in front of us. I remember it like it was yesterday, my husband and I got on the elevator in the hospital leaving the testing area for our baby girl and there was a boy in a wheelchair that was having difficulty speaking, my husband looked at me and said, "There isn't nothing else to worry about, our baby is going to be fine." When you think you have it bad, there is always someone else that has it worse. After a few months of testing, my baby girl was determined to be just fine. God moved that mountain of liver disease.

My marriage went through countless storms, the devil thought he won, but God said NO! Let no man put asunder what God joined together. He even blessed us with another baby boy. Kendrick was a blessing because he came after all the storms, turmoil, and catastrophe and after I lost two sets of twins. Once you learn that marriage is work, you will learn to work the word in your marriage. The devil does not want you to be happy. He comes to steal, kill, and destroy by any means necessary. We as women must learn to guard our marriages in the spiritual realm through prayer and petition. God hears us, but when we entertain the wrong voice and run our mouths to the wrong people about our marriage, the devil has a window of opportunity to manifest within the walls of our home, the compartments of your vehicles, and in the mind of our souls.

Many of the battles we face in our marriages are because we don't pray and guard them from destruction. We speak the wrong things over our marriages and then when they manifest we get angry and blame everyone but ourselves for allowing such behavior to exist. I prayed without ceasing after God reunited us and guess what, one day my husband came and told me that he wanted to be baptized. WHAT! I was shocked and excited, my soul rejoiced. I was overjoyed to hear him say those words, but I prayed for it and God allowed it to happen. Being stationed in Hawaii bought me so much sunshine, I continue to thank God for placing me there.

My prayers after ten years of marriage are very different from the prayers that I prayed before.

"Put on the whole armour of God, that ye may be able to stand against the wiles of the devil. For we wrestle not against flesh and blood, but against principalities, against powers, against the rulers of the darkness of this world, against spiritual wickedness in high places. Wherefore take unto you the whole armour of God, that ye may be able to withstand in the evil day, and having done all, to stand. Stand therefore, having

your loins girt about with truth, and having on the breastplate of righteousness; And your feet shod with the preparation of the gospel of peace;

Above all, taking the shield of faith, wherewith ye shall be able to quench all the fiery darts of the wicked. And take the helmet of salvation, and the sword of the Spirit, which is the word of God: Praying always with all prayer and supplication in the Spirit, and watching thereunto with all perseverance and supplication for all saints; (Ephesians 6:11-18 KJV)."

This very word has blessed my life, my children, and my marriage.

You can't tell me the power of God is weak. He worked a miracle in our lives and I am still here to talk about it. When we pray for one thing and God does another, we must realize that sometimes God's plan for our life isn't our plan. We need to pray and ask God's will to be done and to allow us to move in the direction of His will for us.

In 2010 and for two years, I prayed for a divorce from my husband, but God had a different plan that I knew nothing about. I operated and prayed based on my feelings and the hate I had in my heart. God had to deal with me and He turned things around, according to His will and purpose for our lives. God will separate you to deal with you individually and then reunite you as two fresh people to make things work if it is in His will. If you don't go through anything, you can't have strength to endure the next journey in life. How can I serve You, oh God? I had to learn to change my mindset and then my prayers changed. Much prayer, much power; little prayer, little power. My mom always told me that.

I was specific in my prayers about what I wanted from God. This was one of my prayers.

"Oh, gracious God, I need you now more than ever before. God enter into my space right now and guide me in the direction that you want me to go. Talk to me right now, oh God, I'm listening for Your sweet voice. For You know my every desire as a wife, mother, Soldier, daughter, and friend. You know my needs and my wants for my marriage, oh God. Teach me how to be

a loving wife, a listening wife, a praying wife, a better mother, a listening mother, and a patient mother to my children. Heal my heart, oh God, from the things of the past. Change me, oh God and give me fresh wind. For old things have passed away and today they are new in you. Father, I look to You for whence my help comes from. Show me, oh God, what You want me to do. In Jesus name I pray, Amen."

You must learn to use your power through prayer and petition to turn things around. We have so much power in the words we speak in our own lives and we don't even realize it. Remember, what you speak over yourself will manifest if you believe it.

From out of the heart, the mouth speaks. What do you believe for your life, marriage, relationships, children, friends, and situations? Do you speak negatively all the time? Or do you speak words of affirmation, healing, deliverance and peace? I have learned that if you change the way you think, you change the way you speak. Declare what you want to see and stop speaking negatively over what you really want. Many of us hate on ourselves and wonder why others do the same to us. You can be your best cheerleader, you don't need anyone to validate you because that comes from God. You must know who you are to walk in your purpose and be who God called you to be.

You must read the word of God to tap into the power of God. I use to frown upon Bible study until I began to search for what the Bible was really trying to say. I needed answers and I was tired of trying to figure out the thus, tho, art, and thou words, in their Biblical context. So God planted me at Love First and now I absolutely love Bible study, Sometimes it's how it is being taught that causes us to lose interest, but I was searching for a way ahead because I wanted to know more and understand more about god's instructions for my life. Don't give up on something you really want, keep searching and God will guide you to the right path that will allow you to understand what He is trying to show you. The power of God's hand in your life is priceless and the best answer to all your questions. Don't move through life without it!

CHAPTER THREE

The Waiting Room

In July 2016, I received promotion orders to Master Sergeant in the United States Army. Shortly after, I received orders to Fort Gordon, GA as the Army Reserve Liaison. I was excited, happy, and overwhelmed, yet ready to conquer the world. My happiness was short lived once I shared the news with my husband. This conversation sparked an issue I didn't even know was coming. We had some very tough decisions to make because of our family dynamics at the present time. My husband suffers from post-traumatic stress disorder, my oldest son doesn't handle change very well, and my oldest daughter was undergoing heart procedures and evaluations during this time period.

We decided to delay their move and I would go ahead by myself. Well, you can feel my pain at this point because after all we had been through to reunite our family, here it was again that we would be separated. I prayed and asked God to see me through what I called a storm, but God saw it as a waiting room. Promotion and increase come from God, but at every level of increase there is a giant waiting to slay you. I had no idea who the giant would be, how the giant would look, or if there would be more than one giant. I had to activate my NOW faith and lean all the way on God like I learned to do before. I have never been separated from my children, so this was a very hard pill to swallow for myself, my husband, and my children.

I found an apartment that reminded me of a jail cell. In my mind, all I needed was a place to sleep, eat, and change clothes, so it worked. I moved in and tried my best to make it feel like home, but the H-O-M-E was missing from this place. I went into prayer and meditation mode, letting God speak to my heart, mind, body, and soul. He started to give me tasks to occupy my mind and keep the devil from entering into my space. First, God gave me my sorority contacts. They kept me engaged in community service projects, fellowship, going out to eat, and going to church. God then placed the word, "masters" on my mind. This was something that I vowed never to do because I was sick and tired of school. However, I enrolled into Grand Canyon University's Master's of Leadership program and the light bulb really came on for me.

I started to take a deep dive into an area of study that I realized I was so passionate about. I then became more in tuned with being a liaison for soldiers at my job. I was no longer just a liaison but a game changer, a motivator, a strategist, a mother, a caretaker, and an experienced problem solver. I enjoyed going to Darling Hall, sticking my key in the door, turning it, and knowing that every day is a great day. I had the privilege of changing lives, calming a family member, and making an impact on a Soldier. I assisted in a brighter tomorrow. I gave them hope when they thought it was the end. My smile, my motivation, and my presence was like an alarm to do something different.

I had a gift that God gave me to share with the world and it is my duty to use it to the best of my God-given ability. Even though I enjoyed my job of service and life was looking up, I always thought about my husband and children.

"Why me, God?" I would cry out and asked myself all the time. "Why did you separate me from my family again, Lord?"

I prayed and asked God to hurry up and change my family dynamic so they could move with me. I loved my job but the separation sometimes ate at me. Oh, but when I dropped to my knees in the presence of the Lord, late in the midnight hour and cried out, "Lord help me!" A small, sweet voice would reassure me that trouble wouldn't last always and I would wipe my tears and smile. My NOW faith was kicking in.

God gave me another task that I never knew I could do. I was on Facebook, sharing my pastor's prayer and posting positive messages on a daily basis. I would share my family photos and just display compassion and happiness. One day, God spoke to me.

"Go LIVE and share your experience of being here alone."

I did it and I got an overwhelming response. People were watching that I never knew would be watching. They reached out to me and told me that it touched their life as well. God told me to do it every week, but I ignored that command and didn't do another video until a year later. Just so happens it was the same day as the year before. God always has perfect timing. The exact same thing happened: people were watching and reached out again saying how it impacted their life. Now I hear God loud and clear. This led me to start doing more speaking on Facebook.

One day, my children's aunt reached out and asked me to assist her in a group for domestic violence. I said yes and became a moderator for Cultivating

Clarity in our community for domestic violence. This gave me a platform to become more aware as a domestic violence survivor and counselor, as well as allow me to use my skills and experience as a sexual assault/harassment victim advocate. Look how God was moving in my life! All while I was upset about being separated from my family, God was moving in my waiting room.

As I was working in the Facebook groups teaching classes about different topics related to domestic violence, I saw my children's aunt post about an upcoming anthology project she was leading. The We Are Women of Substance Anthology was compiled by 10 fabulous women of substance. I knew this was God because after all I'd been through, he placed this on Star's heart to share. I jumped right on it. This project became near and dear to my heart because it allowed me to go back in time and really take a deep dive into what situations and circumstances grew me into a woman of substance. What is a woman of substance? I had to answer that question by talking about each pivotal point that changed my life in such a way that I became a better woman, mother, wife and friend. Now, I am a published author. God was working things out for me and I loved every minute of it. Putting my journey on paper solidified my purpose. It explained the pain and how it was used to birth a vision that would ultimately lead to my destiny.

It was through my Be-Still-And-Know time with God that I started to hear His voice more clearly and moved in the direction of my most dominant thought. To be still allows you to pause, ponder, pray, and most importantly listen to God's direction for your life. The knowing part comes with your understanding of God's time, his guidance, and each path he sets before you. Being obedient is the action part of knowing when God is speaking to you. Pausing to meditate and be still was very hard for me at first, but every week I learned to sit longer and longer. We get to choose what we pay attention to. We get to choose what we focus on and what we react to. While writing my chapter for the anthology, I kept hearing a voice say, "What about your own book that you stopped writing?" So, I opened my manuscript for this very book and picked up where I left off.

I had to set a date and that date was July 30, 2018, I changed it to November 30, 2018, and then it changed to December 31, 2018. This book has to be finished before then, so all the other things that have to get done in order to publish it has to happen. Now I set a date, it gave me a sense of urgency, and all my accountability partners are holding me to what I said. God paused my book because of the storm I was currently in. There was no way the book could get published without the current storm in it.

I wrestled with procrastination at points in my life, but that doesn't mean it's a bad idea or you should scrap it. There were so many things happening in my waiting room that I got distracted and forgot what God initially told me to do. Even though I set a date and it passed, I didn't scrap it, I just paused it. July 30th then turned into November 30th and guess what, the book is finished and off to the editor. I said all that to say this, seek God's guidance on things you have put on pause. If it remains a relevant part of your destiny, you will get it done.

I have allowed my NOW faith to change me. I didn't even realize the change until I stopped and looked back one day. I stopped and looked at the people on my social media sites, I stopped and looked at my pictures and saw the change for myself. When I stopped and looked backwards, I noticed the old me had evolved into showing the God in me. My circle changed, the people I spoke to changed, and I noticed it by who had deleted themselves, hid themselves and who was still standing with me. God placed me in the waiting room of Augusta, GA to birth the vision and purpose he had for my life. However, as I navigated through my waiting room, the devil appeared when I wasn't quite paying attention. I knew things had changed for me, but I didn't realize that because I started walking with God and for God that the devil would try to run me off the road in plain sight.

"No!" I heard God say before I saw a devil from my past in person. I saw a person that used to be my friend appear and God reminded me of the horrible journey she took and it landed her in hot water. That was my notice that destruction was coming, but I did not heed the warning. I ignored the flashing yellow caution light and continued to travel as if I knew what was coming, but I really didn't.

My nephew was gunned down in the streets of Chicago, my mom passed and I was an emotional wreck trying to mask it with other things. I never sought help and this allowed my mind to be clouded and not think clearly on my job. I made a decision under pressure to ignore God and it placed me in hot water. This was a test of my NOW FAITH once again. Will I trust God to keep me safe or will I be afraid and worry about what the Army will do with my career? I chose to increase my NOW faith and lean all the way on God. I am human and I make mistakes, but God forgave me. He went before me and covered me during the storm I placed myself in. I have never been so mad at myself, but I forgave myself and asked God to forgive me and now I am walking in God's footsteps to get to the other side of this storm. This too shall pass. God blessed me with a second chance. He knew my heart and He knew the decision I would make, but the thing about God is that He loves me anyway.

I basically took the heat for something I did not do, but all fingers were pointing at me, so as a leader I took a stand to take all the heat rounds because it was ultimately for me anyway. Someone told me they could help me and instead of me asking a bunch of questions I figured it was covered and I turned in my documents and kept on moving. I now know how political life is at the top of the food chain and if you have a target on your back, then they will take you down no matter what.

It is decision time, the Criminal Investigation Division investigation concluded, the Commander gave his recommendation, and the CG prepared to meet with me to give me the verdict. All punishment suspended is what I heard, but apparently everyone else in the room heard something different. However, I left the room thanking God and being so grateful.

Through my entire investigation period, I felt disconnected from my team members, especially my Sergeant Major whom I felt was racist towards me from the day I met him. I also felt he didn't have my best interest at heart. He was trying his best to find anything to bring me down. His number one priority became to stop Master Sergeant Gore by any means necessary. While I was going through this storm, I had a corrective surgery on my left hand and elbow. I got 30 days convalescent leave to spend at home with my family and I loved every bit of it.

Once I returned back to Fort Gordon, the heart ache started again. So did the mess from my command. Now they wanted me to perform extra duty for 21 days and that was not annotated on my documents. My documents did not match their documents and they couldn't believe it. After going back to them several times, they finally stated that I received a bad copy. That is what they said and the extra duty stands. So, they get to make mistakes but I don't, noted. The duty started before I was cleared from my doctor, so when I went to the doctor they placed me on seven day quarters. I got really sick mid-week and had to return to the ER on Thursday because of stomach problems. To my surprise and for the first time ever since I had been stationed here, my entire command group came to the hospital. They said they came because they were concerned, but I didn't believe them. They were being nosey and wanted to see what was going on with me. I felt harassed and violated because they all showed up unannounced. They even started speaking with the doctor, asking him questions about me, which is a violation of HIPAA.

After my ER visit, I got a knock on my door. Three men were at my door asking me to come outside and talk to them. They said that they were concerned about my health and welfare. I went and sat at the apartment park benches and the Colonel called the Commander and we had a conversation about me coming to see him on Monday to discuss my whereabouts over the weekend. They claimed that they were so worried about my mental health and my welfare that they just had to come see me, but my truth is different.

They are attacking me and trying their best to destroy my career. Yes, I made a mistake that I owned up to and I got my punishment for that, now leave me alone. They are watching me like a private and following me around because I matter so much, really? They see the anointing on my life and they can't stand it, so they will try and take me down at all cost. My family doesn't matter to them and neither do I. I am simply just another black number and they want to get rid of me because of my greatness. See, punishment isn't the same for everyone, I found out that color matters, who you know matters, and if you're kissing up to people in charge, that matters. Well, the only person I got is God on my side.

They are now trying to do something else, something is brewing, but I don't know what. They are also trying to prevent me from taking leave for my graduation, my son's birthday, and my book signing. The enemy always comes to steal, kill, and destroy. I have done great things for the military over the last 19 years and they are merely trying their best to take me down. It is one thing to protect the interest of the military, yet another to antagonize, stalk, and mentally attack a person. But God!

The assignment I was given to come to Augusta alone was a test of my faith in God. The devil was very busy and I had to enter into a spiritual battle. I had to pray without ceasing to guard my entire family with the armour of God. Did I ever have doubts? Yes! That's when I realized I wasn't doing what God said and that is not to worry. I had to reach out for help from like-minded people in spiritual prayer that could stand in the gap for me. I could not have gotten through this tumultuous time without God and people standing with and praying for me. So much was happening to me all at once, that a few times I wanted to just throw in the towel, but the God I serve kept the right people talking to me to keep me on my feet.

Sometimes, negative thoughts would enter my mind and that's when I started to pray as well. I have learned that I can only control me. I had to focus on what I can do in my own strength and give God everything else. I've learned to cast away what I can't or shouldn't carry. I've also learned how to not allow my mistakes and my past to consume me. I must admit it's hard when you know how one mistake could cost you so much, especially on your way out of the military and transitioning into civilian life. Every mistake has a consequence. However, every time I think about it, God asks me why am I concerned with having to explain anything? They won't care about the specifics of the case, all they see is an accusation/charge on my record because I was questioned and investigated by the Criminal Investigative Division (CID).

I keep replaying the investigation and the outcome in my mind and every time I do it, God asks me why am I concerned with my record? I believe that I won't even need my record for the place where God is taking me next. God has me going through these chain of events for my good. He didn't say it would feel good, but it's going to work out for my good. God is magnificent all by Himself and every time I question anything, He asks me why am I concerned with it in the first place. If it's in my life, I can handle it.

God told me to wait and let Him move on my behalf, but I sat thinking about this entire ordeal and the person that helped me never said a word, never batted an eye, never said anything. Little did I know someone was in the shadows with the truth and finally spoke up, but it still didn't matter. I realized that because I had a mark on me for greatness, I was under a spiritual attack. It was orchestrated to make me go crazy, get depressed, steal my joy, and cause me discomfort. However, the God I serve knew it was coming before I did and just simply told me to be still and know. The same Sergeant Major that went to CID in the first place came to me and claimed he wanted to have a genuine conversation. However, it was really more of the same, he just tried to sugar coat it this time. Racism is real in the Army and although they claim to have a policy in place to handle it, but you still need the right skin color for the right protection. I saw everything unfold right before my eyes and still they tried to act like it wasn't anything racist going on.

I believe the command was not happy with the outcome from the first case, so now they are investigating me again for not being at home when they came to my house. This is just to cause me more stress, anguish, and pain. This is just a momentary, light affliction and this too shall pass. I never knew why many senior non-commissioned officers got out before they made Sergeant Major, but now I see. Grace from man in the military is only given to whom they like, but God gives grace every day.

I have learned valuable lessons in this waiting room. The most valuable of them all is for me not to lean on my own understanding, but to trust in the Lord with all my heart. Another lesson is for me to be still and know God is who He said He is. God has had me waiting several times through this entire season. In the CID office, through the investigation process I had to wait. Through the punishment phase on extra duty I have been waiting for time to pass. Now under another investigation, I am waiting again. Patience is a virtue.

I'm really trying to understand how I made it 19 years before the dog and pony show started happening to me. I saw it happen to others I knew, but never in a million years did I think it would happen to me. These incidents only confirm that I have a greater calling on my life and now it's time to accept a transition. Some places in life are only for a season and if we push to stay, things will start happening that force us to move on. I definitely believe that's how God works. His plan is greater than our plan. I'm not a problematic person. I have never been in trouble my entire career until I got here to the place many call doom. I owned my mistake, but I will not carry the burden of something I did not do.

I had to focus my energy. Previously, I spoke about meditation. I found the perfect music to sit still and listen. This very act was extremely hard when I first started. Thoughts were racing through my mind to do something. Get up, get my phone, turn on the television, scratch my back, scratch my nose...the list goes on. Lots of thoughts came and went during my first few sessions. The first time I think I only sat still for one minute, but that was a start. You have to be willing to start somewhere. Eventually, I made it to 5 minutes, and then 10 minutes, and now I am at 30 minutes of stillness.

Being still and listening has allowed me to calm the inner noise and the outside chatter. I have now created energy for me to block the noise and listen in silence to God's voice and what He wants me to do for Him and the kingdom. I have heard Him speak to me through this stillness that I can now appreciate. I didn't understand at first but now my thoughts, feelings, and desires are being molded for God's glory. I have shifted my mindset to work on things of God and my purpose-driven life. However, I am not mistake free. I still have to guard myself against making the wrong decisions. The enemy now knows that I turned from my wicked ways and he is still trying to stop me from greatness.

Being able to meditate has given me a new perspective and position in the spiritual realm of my life. I now understand that quietness calms the mind, it allows me to resist the negative thoughts and focus my energy on positive moments in time, as I breath in and out and release the pressures of life. Try it, you will feel a ton of relief, just by breathing calmly alone. Being able to channel your energy on positive thinking and loose the negative chatter is so powerful, it has literally changed my perspective on life. I am now able to think before I speak and pause, ponder, and pray before I react. This is all a direct result of learning to meditate and understand the power within the element of being still.

While you live your life from day to day, you should know that trouble will come your way. However, the Bible tells us that you will have tribulations, but be of good cheer and count it all joy. If we know that battles are coming our way, we have to realize that ahead of time and guard our hearts from it and make sure that we stand ready to combat whatever the enemy forces bring up against us.

Being in the waiting room gave me a lot of time to pause and allow the reality of my actions to set in. I went through several tumultuous times during my waiting room season and I learned a lot. No matter who I am and what I have accomplished, I can still be brought down to the lowest level and have to humble myself. Going through this process doesn't always feel good. God tells us that we will go through things and they may not feel good. Trials and tribulations bring a lesson and we must be able to pass that lesson in order to to move on to the next life lesson. I am a firm believer that God wants us to learn for our greater good, so He allows tribulation to pass through His hands and reach us so that we can have a better understanding on where we are headed. I know that I am headed towards my destiny, so I know that I had to go through each event that has happened to me in order for me to appreciate my destiny.

CHAPTER FOUR

I Love Being A Mother

Often times I think about when I first became a mother and all I can think about is the feeling of life growing inside of my body and how it gave me hope. The feeling of a little fist pushing on my belly made me smile. I was excited to find out that I was pregnant, but I was also afraid because I wasn't home in Chicago. I fled the city because I was shot at and I was in unfamiliar territory and pregnant by someone I just met a few months prior.

In 2002, my first child was born early due to bradycardia. They told me that he had trouble breathing and was trapped inside of my canal and that's why they rushed me to have a C-section after I hadn't dilated. Despite complications, he was the most handsome little fella I could have ever met. I loved on him the way I wanted to be loved. I breast fed him and did everything my doctor told me to do because I wanted the best for him. They told me my son would have developmental delays from loss of oxygen and being born premature, but God.

I spoiled my son, nursed my son, and did the best I could do as a mother. I did this despite my role as a Soldier, my mother's caretaker, and being in a violent relationship with my son's father. We were both young and I wanted my son to have both his parents and was willing to sacrifice my happiness for it. Almost two years passed and things got worse. Through the ups and downs, the turmoil, and make-up sex, I became pregnant again.

He left while I was pregnant because things were just horrible between us. That was no way for me to live. I always knew I could be a great mom. I didn't want to do it alone, but I did. I asked God to help me with my first born and He gave us everything I needed with little to no help from his father. My children's dad re-appeared in December 2004, on the day my second child was born, my lovely daughter. I thought we would be able to give it another shot, but a few months later the turmoil was back to visit. I decided at that point that we should separate and move on without each other. I moved out of my mother's house and into an apartment to separate myself from the mess going on with my children's father. He started harassing and following me. Eventually, he got the picture and left the state. I continued caring for my little family and met another man who captured my heart. I didn't give myself time to heal or prepare for Mr. Right, I just jumped into the next thing smoking!

It took some time, but as I prayed and asked God to give me a permanent position as a Soldier, He allowed me to make my transition to a more peaceful environment. I got a full-time job as a Soldier and I no longer needed food stamps and the WIC program. I was grateful for receiving that assistance because Lord knows I needed it. Through prayer and petition, God gave me the things I needed to support me and my children as I walked by faith and not by sight.

I could no longer move alone. I had to think and make decisions based on my two children and me. This was the fun part that allowed me to be the best mother I could be. However, in the pit of my stomach I still felt I was missing something that I knew nothing about- loving unconditionally. I knew what I was supposed to do for my children and they never wanted for anything. I was a Soldier who traveled a lot, so I started being away from them a lot and I felt a part of my love was dissolving.

I had a decent childhood, despite being sexually abused by a family member, going through the tragic loss of my father being shot, and dealing with the lack of a loving embrace from my adoptive mom. I never got that "welcome home" embrace after visiting family. I never felt the extra special attention, I was just well taken care of. I recreated that environment for my children subconsciously and didn't realize it until they started getting older. I used to wonder why I didn't like holding my daughter's hand in the grocery store. It was because I had no connection like that with my mother or father to mimic. My first two children got the worst of it, even though they didn't realize it. When I discovered what I was doing, I asked God to fix it and show me how to be a more loving mother. I was hurt and broken from my failed relationships, loneliness, and lack of love from my family. All I knew how to do was survive, not only for me, but for my children as well. I never even wanted them to know how bad I was hurting, how lonely I really was, and how unloved I felt.

While trying to stay afloat and keep moving, I started another relationship with a man that made me laugh all the time. We dated for a while and my kids seemed to like him. I got pregnant with my third child but neither of us were ready. As a matter of fact, he had a baby on the way by his current baby momma. I didn't feel like I was going to be with him in the long run, so in 2005 I aborted my child in fear of being alone to care for more children without a father. God spoke to me about it and I felt like I made the worst decision ever, but it was too late to turn the clock back and keep my baby.

I went through a season of self-blame, hurt, anxiety, and depression because, once again, I didn't feel loved. I had two living children that needed me and this helped me bounce back from the funk I was living in. In a confused state of mind, I began doing what I knew best and that was working hard, loving my children, and providing for them. All I wanted to do was provide for my children and make sure they never wanted for anything. That's what my mom and dad showed me and so I did just that.

In 2007, I was still dating the same man I was pregnant by in 2005 and now I was pregnant again with twins. I was so excited, but we were in an on-again, off-again relationship that was driving me insane. I loved this man but he didn't have his life together and I accepted it because I just wanted to be loved and cared for and he was doing that when he was with me. Even though we lived together, things started to get very confusing and unorthodox. He had previously lived with the mother of his last two children, so he was basically taking care of two households. I stopped seeing him after too many arguments about it and this caused my depression again.

During the course of my pregnancy, I made a conscience decision to give up on my on welfare and just do whatever I wanted to do. I developed gestational diabetes and I stopped taking care of myself. I stopped going to my doctors appointments and basically ate and drank whatever I wanted to because I felt like the father of my children didn't really care any way. I really didn't even care. I used to go out of my way to go visit him and be with him and make things work, but he did whatever he wanted to do because we weren't married. His philosophy was that if he wasn't married, he could do what he wanted to do. That was the first sign of a dysfunctional relationship that I glossed over.

In February 2007, I lost my twins. They passed abruptly due to my placenta bursting and my blood pressure being extremely high. I had preeclampsia for several days without even going to the hospital because I didn't think anyone cared. I should have been the one caring, despite what the father of my children was doing. I totally ignored my health because I was in love and depressed. Nothing was going according to what I planned. I gave up on my health and the protection of my babies because my man wasn't acting right. He didn't care until I called him and told him that our babies had passed away. That was a bad decision that I made. I allowed the lack of control to take over my mind and I now have to live with that understanding.

On August 9, 2008, after all of the depression, turmoil, and the loss of our babies, we got married. This was a very happy and exciting time in my life. Six weeks later I found out I was pregnant with another baby girl. She was born May 7, 2009. My baby girl was pretty active in my belly and it seemed like she just wanted to burst out and be here to celebrate with us. This was a very healthy pregnancy for me despite being put on bed rest because her head had dropped down low. She came out fighting and ready to conquer the world. Chloe came just as I graduated from DeVry with my Bachelor's degree and just as we were transitioning to another state. She gave me a breath of fresh air and another reason why God saved my life. Chloe was my cry baby, she cried all the time because she wanted more love, affection, food, and whatever she wanted, when she wanted it. Chloe definitely reminded me of myself and I wondered if I too was a cry baby.

In 2010, My husband deployed to get away from the heat of our marriage and just as I discovered I was pregnant again with twins. God gave me another set of twins and I was excited. I did everything the doctor asked me to do, until week ten when I found out I had twin-twin transfusion and needed surgery to fix it.

I was scared. I was lonely. I called on God. I only had my mother to lean on and no one else. I wanted my babies to live so bad, but I was scared. I finally reached a place where I was obedient to God and doing everything the doctor said. They flew me to the Fetal Care Center of Cincinnati in Ohio. My husband met me there.

The surgery was successful. I still believed that God was going to make sure my babies were alright. I was being as careful as I could and trying to stay off my feet as much as possible. The doctors checked me daily and discovered an infection. My water bag started leaking and the doctors said I developed vaginosis. Knowing I had sex with my husband days prior, I knew it has to come from that. I sucked up my emotional turmoil and prayed, asking God to intervene. My husband had one choice to make and he made the wrong one. He chose to fly back to Iraq and I flew home alone, you heard me all alone when he had the opportunity to go with me to make sure I was okay. In my opinion, that was an automatic divorce.

The next few weeks were very difficult for me. I was on bed rest, hoping that the leak would stop and seal itself. The doctors told me either it would stop or I would go into active labor. I needed to be at least 22 weeks in order for them to save their lives. On December 19, after hearing a dog bark for a very long time, I got up to see what was happening. As I watched the dog break through the fence, my water bag busted and I went into active labor. I knew in my heart that was the end, but I called 911 and asked for help any way. When I arrived at the hospital, my doctor said there was nothing we could do but push through the birth. He could not save their lives. I gave birth to two living children that I watched die in my mother's arms. Again, I was devastated, alone, confused, and very hurt. My living children, Malik, Makiyah, and Chloe, were small but they knew what was happening and tried to console me as best they could.

Preparing for the funeral was heart wrenching for me and I was depressed all over again. This time I had my mom, my children, and my unit team members who assisted and stepped up to help me any way they could. They showed up and showed out for me and my family. I thank God for stationing me with such a wonderful team. I was upset with God, but He brought me through this time as well. He gave me some remarkable people to lean on and help me get back on my feet. I appreciate each of them for it.

I filed for a divorce and wanted to move on with my life. I could not allow someone to mistreat me and disrespect me any longer. I begged my job to move me to another location so that I could heal and thrive. God answered my prayers and relocated me to paradise; Hawaii. Life began to be peaceful, but a struggle for my children. Chloe missed her father. I struggled too, but things needed to change and we could not carry on as such.

We were doing great in Hawaii with our new beginning. As my mom prayed for some sort of divine intervention, I prayed for God to move my divorce as fast as possible so I could just move on. Well, I was praying against God's will for my life and after a year-long court case, God reunited my husband and I after two years of separation, counseling, and phone conversations to figure out what was next.

We made the connection and agreed to get back together. As we were dating again, I found out I was pregnant again. Yes, again! I flew to Indonesia on a trip with my job and realized that something wasn't right but I kind of overlooked it. When I got back home I went to get a check-up and the doctor told me I was 8 weeks pregnant. God had blessed us with another baby. I was on pins and needles, scared to death thinking God was going to take this baby from me as well. Once again, I followed the doctor's orders and did everything they told me to do. They treated me as high risk due to my past. We all were very cautious. I had a pretty good pregnancy with my little love child. All while I was pregnant I saw rainbows, so I figured that God was giving me a sign that all was going to be okay.

In November 2013, my last child, Kendrick K. C. Gore, was born. It felt like he had already been here before. Our baby boy blessed our lives and gave us a new perspective on things. He is definitely the salt in our house. Each of my children are unique in their own way. Each one has given me a new way of looking at my life. I have learned to be a better mother each time God allowed me to get pregnant. The pain of aborting one and losing four is unbearable, but it taught me a valuable lesson. I should have been focused on God through all my pregnancies, but I was focused on a man making me feel a certain way. I should have paid more attention to my children and not worry about the stressors of life and what someone else was doing. I made mistakes along the way and it didn't bring my children back, but it gave me four powerful souls that love me unconditionally. No matter what happens, they will always love me and I will always love them.

Being a mother has allowed me to love and show my affection, the same love and affection I seek from a man. I've learned throughout the years how to get better at being a mom and loving myself unconditionally because I didn't have all the right answers at first. I allowed how I was treated as a daughter to play a factor in how I treated my children. God showed me what I was doing and how to do it better. Motherhood is learned through trial and error and reading and learning how to do things a different way. I never wanted to treat my children how I was treated. When you learn better, you are supposed to do better. Don't keep recycling the same generational foolishness because that's all you know. Get in groups, talk to people that are doing what's right, go to the doctor, and get some assistance. There are lots of ways to learn more and do a better job than what was done to you. Let those excuses go. The only real excuse that holds you back is you!

The abortion taught me that I was being selfish and I allowed the spirit of death to enter into my life. I never casted it down until recently. If you have ever faced an abortion, please make sure you talk to God and cast that spirit of death out of your life. I did not realize the effects of the spirit of abortion until now. It carries a heaven burden in your life and even when you think you are doing the right thing, it's the spirit that lives within the crevices of your very soul. It must be cleansed and released from your body as well as your spiritual realm. You must be cleansed inside and out so that you can bring back the blessings that were killed off by the abortion.

Every pregnancy showed me that each life is uniquely developed and molded to perform a different task in your life. I love each of my children and I pour into them as God allows me to. I don't know a perfect mother, but love is very strong and it will stand the test of time. As a mother, I didn't start off with the right perspective, but I gradually gained my footing and adapted to the changes in my life, whether I caused them or not. The lack of self-love I faced played a very intricate part in me not taking care of myself and allowing the behavior of a man to consume my thoughts. Do not allow a person to engulf your life so much that you forget about yourself and who you are and the life that you carry. I had to seek help for that and I am grateful that help was available. Never be too proud to say "I need help." It took me a while to understand it, but sometimes you don't get the lesson until something as tragic as losing a life happens and then the lesson hits you head on.

It is a joy and an honor for me to be the mother of seven wonderful children in our blended family. I have four biological children and three by marriage. Every time we go out we have a good ole time. I love spoiling our children, teaching our children, having meaningful conversations with our children, and exploring life with our children. I really enjoy the family outings, parties, vacations, trips, and game nights together. As they grow older I notice that they aren't interested in all the lovie dovie stuff we used to do. They aren't always up under me like they used to be. They just want money to shop. God allowed me to be a mother to teach me patience, unconditional love, how to be supportive, humble, and affectionate. All the things I was searching for in a man after the death of my father. I thank God for giving me such an honor and a privilege because not everyone can be a mother. I go above and beyond to ensure my children are well taken care of. I knew how to financially support my children from the start, but God took me through some situations to allow me to learn the rest.

I am a firm believer that if you never go through anything, you won't know how to respond to adversity. Mothers face adversity and it is defined as circumstances and conditions that cause anguish, affliction, stress, physical discomfort, heart ache, pain, and psychological destruction. These all can be counterattacked through the power of prayer as a mother. Our children will go through things that we feel as if it is happening to us, such as medical issues and trouble they may face. We have to know how to war in the spirit to place a hedge of protection around ourselves and our children. I think of myself today as a prayer warrior and I intercede on behalf of myself, my marriage, my children, and everyone connected to me by blood. It is through the power of prayer that the tide turned in all the situations I mentioned above. I cannot tell you enough that you need to pray in the spiritual realm and constantly pray without ceasing.

I leave you with this, being a mother is the most exciting and rewarding job I have held since my existence. Embrace every moment with your children, especially while they are young. I lost some very important times being a Soldier and being called to duty. I can never get those times back, but God allowed me to create new memories and exciting moments to have forever in my memory bank. If you don't know the answer, seek wise counsel concerning your children. What someone else does with or for their children, may not benefit your life as a mother. Talk to God about it, He will lead and guide you down the right path.

    I have read books on motherhood, talked to other mothers, pastors, medical staff, my family etc., when I didn't have the answers. Things work out when you seek wise counsel, but if you don't they can lead to a very dark place. Don't allow your children to divide your household, they come after your husband or wife in divine order. Discipline your children so that they don't become unruly and overthrow your home. You must set rules and a direction for your children to grow and become healthy and respectful citizens of this world. Lastly, love them with the love of the Lord. Never compare them to one another because it only causes division amongst them all. I pray that this chapter has blessed you in some way, shape, or form. Be Blessed!

CHAPTER FIVE

Adopted

I was raised by my father, K.C. Blandin, and adoptive mother, Annie Blandin. They both loved me and cared for me. I didn't have a worry in this world. Although I was well taken care of, I always wanted to know why my mother gave me up for adoption.

When I was in elementary school, I learned that my biological mother was a woman I thought was my auntie. I didn't know how to feel back then. I used to visit her house and spend time with her, so why was I given up for adoption and living elsewhere? This is a question that has gone unanswered for 36 years. Or maybe I should say, I never got the entire answer.

On Mother's Day 2015, I told God that I was tired of asking and just accepted the fact that I was never going to get the answer I deserved. The last time I asked, my biological mother told me that it was because my dad was in a better position than she was. That answer never satisfied me. Even though I was in a home where I was well taken care of, I was molested by a family member for three years. Even though I was showered with financial love and a home of love, I always wondered why I was adopted. The person I wanted to tell me the truth never did and it really hurt my feelings. This trauma has caused me to live out my anger and push my biological mother to the side. Yes, I took care of her and she came and helped me raise my children when I was going through hell with my husband and after we reunited as well. I looked out for her and she looked out for me, but for years it was a very silent and distant relationship under the same roof.

I mistreated my mom, yelled at her and at times, didn't even want to see her because of my anger and pain. I had to take it to God to give me a new heart to see things differently despite never getting resolution. God is now strengthening my relationship with my biological mother through the spirit of forgiveness. I had to be willing to release the hurt or carry it and be mad forever. Being mad forever was causing problems with my children. I didn't want them to see me get angry and disgruntled all the time. I never want my children to treat me how I treated my mom. I had a reality check of my very own. I had to look at myself in the mirror and understand my own rage and outlandish behavior towards my mother. It was deeply rooted in a love I always wanted, a relationship I never had, the pain I felt inside as a little girl longing for her biological mother.

No one is perfect. So, I took a step back to look at the bigger picture. There is a reason why I was adopted that no one seems to want me to know about, but God knows and He wants me to do right by my children. Due to all of the hell I went through as a child, teenager, and young adult, I could not see the good in the situation. I was carrying the hurt and pain everywhere instead of casting it out.

How many of you are carrying feelings of abandonment, hurt, shame, or guilt? Cast it out! It only hardens your heart. I needed my heart to be right because I have children to raise and I want them to see a better example. So, change my heart, God. Make it ever true. Change my heart, God. Make it more like You! Change me, oh God. This verse in Tamela Mann's "Change Me," became my prayer. I love it because God has truly changed me, one season at a time. I thank God for my mom coming into my life and helping me love on my children. Many people don't have a second chance at it, but God gave me one. I am blessed to have had two mothers that both love me unconditionally.

I learned a very valuable lesson through it all. It's not where you come from, it's where you're going. We all must make a dent with our dash; the little line between our birth date and death. Even though my life began one way, there is no excuse for me not using the gift God gave me to reach my destiny. My story started with me being birthed, then adopted and going through some very tumultuous seasons, but that is not how my story has to end. God equipped us all with a brain to gain knowledge and use that knowledge as power to turn the course of our lives for His glory. I did not understand that until I developed a close relationship with God. God showed me that I had a hardened heart towards my mom and I had to see it first and acknowledge it before I was able to deal with it, despite me wanting answers. After being in arguments and seeing the rage and bad attitudes, I decided that things needed to change. It was not an immediate change, but it all started with me confessing from my mouth "I forgive you, Mom," period. From that very day a relationship door opened in order for us to start over and begin a life of love despite the past. God said, all things passed away, become new. I had to embrace it. It has been a long road, but things are turning around for the good.

Pray this prayer if you ever have faced a situation such as mine.

--The Serenity Prayer--
God grant me the serenity to accept the things I cannot change;
courage to change the things I can; and wisdom to know the difference.
Living one day at a time;
Enjoying one moment at a time;
Accepting hardships as the pathway to peace;
Taking, as He did, this sinful world as it is, not as I would have it;
Trusting that He will make all things right if I surrender to His Will;
That I may be reasonably happy in this life and supremely happy with Him
Forever in the next. Amen.

CHAPTER SIX

Faith Fight

Have you ever thought about giving up? Throwing in the towel? Committing suicide? Well, I have answered yes to each of those questions once or twice in my life. I can tell you that as long as I operated on autopilot, my life was in turmoil. I made bad decisions by not including God at all. I was captivated by the world and what people thought, ultimately sinking in sadness.

Every season I have gone through in my life was on purpose. They were meant to strengthen me and give me the tools for my greater calling which is to speak, motivate, teach, and train others. I have been in a true faith fight since April 2018. God shows me when I am wrong and I am forced to deal with me.

Following the deaths of my nephew, my mother and my brother, my mind was twisted with lies and deceit. I had to turn my life back over to God. I was under stress from being away from my children and husband, living alone in Augusta. I had so much on my plate that I made a decision to ask a person that was not in the right position to help me get an extension on my basic housing allowance for six more months at my job and it cost my mental stability and my health. There was a correct protocol I should have followed, but I took what seemed to be an easier route considering the person knew my situation and offered assistance. I owned my mistake, but did not want to get others involved so I took the entire hit and humbled myself to be subject to whatever punishment I was about to face.

I began to wonder what God was up to, but I instantly recognized that I was in a faith fight. God wanted to see if I was ready after all he had taken me through and the answer was yes. I was more than equipped to handle my next season. So, He started revealing each task I needed to complete as I proved to Him that I could handle my next destination.

During my entire military career, I fought, learned, got promoted, and climbed the ladder of success because I was chasing the rank of Sergeant Major. I knew that I was a good leader, but I always strived to be a great leader. I've only had two great mentors in my military career and both of them saw me as an excellent leader. However, the journey I placed myself on has now diverted me to my destiny. The Army gave me a platform to learn, grow, and make the necessary mistakes I needed so that God could elevate me to my destiny. Through every storm I have encountered here at Fort Gordon, I have grown into who God wants me to be.

A faith fight is a fight in the spiritual realm. It is a battle you can only fight through much prayer and the power of the Holy Spirit. Have you ever went into your closet, dropped to your knees, and started praying? I have and now I do it every chance I get. It is necessary to fight your battles in the spiritual realm because that controls the earthly realm. If you are not interceding on your behalf, try it. You can move your mountain by simply praying and fasting. Speak directly to your mountain instead of talking about your mountain. I never knew how to fight spiritually until I got my own home, went through marriage troubles, health battles, etc. These things caused me to get my relationship with God right. Once I started, I couldn't stop. I also pray at midnight because when the devil thinks we are sleeping, he is up causing trouble.

My faith fight showed me that I was ready for my new journey because all the other times I went through a faith fight, I was depressed, sad, disgruntled, unkind, pissed off, angry, and just overwhelmed. This season was different. I was scared because I didn't have any of the feelings I just mentioned. I wondered why I was so calm through the storms. I was very aware of my situation and circumstances and I know God was there with me in that moment. My response shocked me, but I knew in the back of my mind that it was my responsibility to be calm in the storm. I cannot allow the enemy to cause me to act a fool. That was the old me. The old me would have blown a gasket, but God sat with me and told me to relax. He assured me that it would work out for my good. I received the message and knew that this season gave me a voice of honesty, clarity, competence, and calmness.

The beginning of 2018 was rough for me. By April, there was so much going on. I wasn't thinking clearly and moved in the midst of chaos at home, work, family, and in my mind. You never know what type of decisions you will make until you are placed in a tumultuous season. I thought I had it all together when a hurricane hit my life. One death after another, my marriage on the rocks, children struggling in school, and I was separated from my family. My family was going through hell because of my promotion to E8- Master Sergeant. I believe all of this was a test to see if I was resilient. Yes, I passed that test. When we ask for one thing, God may give it to us and also show us why it wasn't such a big grand idea to have it in our lives. Sometimes, God just wants to teach us a lesson in it all. I have definitely had my fair share of lessons and tumultuous seasons.

My mind set was much different than it was back in 2007. I had all the tools to win. I had resources, meditation, a pastor, a church family, and now my husband and children as motivation. God amazed me when He got my husband involved on a whole other level. My husband started going to church on Saturday for Men Stepping Up. He even started going to the doctor to heal. My oldest son started getting good grades as a sophomore and I gained a band of women that wanted me to win. God took away my bad seeds and gave me beautiful flowers as friends and women in Christ. I am grateful and honored to be connected to excellence.

CHAPTER SEVEN

The United States Army

On October 18, 1999, I joined the United States Army Reserves. Ready, willing and able to accept responsibility, I was so excited to join one of the most powerful forces of all times. I originally set out to join the Active Army because I loved the Junior Reserve Officer Training Course (JROTC) so much and I knew I had it in me to be a leader. I was destined for greatness from the very start of my life, but I didn't realize it then. All I knew was that I was ready for the world. I had a strong and powerful voice and I loved the systematic characteristics that the Army had to offer.

My mother signed off on my paperwork because she saw my passion and was excited for me. My dad had already passed away by then. My father always told me that I would only join the Army over his dead body and that actually came true. I shipped out to basic training after my mom suffered a stroke. I didn't want to leave her, but I signed the contract. That meant I could only delay it, but I would eventually have to go. I was sad to leave my mom, but excited about the new journey I was beginning. I could picture the drill sergeants screaming and yelling and it was just like I pictured in my mind. I spoke to God about it before I got there and asked him to cover me and get me through. I had no idea how good I really was until the end of my career. I was as a Soldier, leader, trainer, motivator, counselor, friend, battle buddy, subordinate, peer, and senior leader. All while I was hustling and bustling through life, making decisions that would allow me to get promoted by God to the next level in my career, changes were happening inside of me. Miracles were being performed inside of me and a strong, black woman was birthed. My relationship with God was created and secured. I became a mother, wife, and divine sister. I wanted to be a Soldier, but in the process God allowed me to be so much more.

The Army gave me the opportunity to learn, grow, excel, teach, train, motivate, and counsel Soldiers to the best of my ability. I have been given the opportunity of a lifetime to gain pertinent information, skills, abilities, and learn many different life lessons to propel me into the woman I am today. I am very thankful and grateful for this opportunity given to me by God. I know I have touched many lives along the way and for that, I smile. I believe God put me on this path to prepare me for my next journey, my destiny, and my ultimate God-given purpose. Every tool and resource I have gained in the Army is and will always be very valuable in pursuit of my destiny.

Leadership, Duty, Respect, Selfless Service, Honor, Integrity, and Personal courage are the seven

Army values that have guided my entire military career in addition to God's hand upon my life. I took what the Army taught me and used it to achieve my goals within the leadership realm. Leadership has always been at the forefront of my destiny, even before I realized it.

Trust is earned and so is respect. I learned to trust and respect some great people during my tenure in the Army. I gained so much knowledge from listening and allowing some of my leaders to touch my life in a very impactful way. I have learned through the good times and bad times, mistakes and all. Without me going through something I would never have the resilience I have right now. The thoughts crossed my mind to give up, but God turned it around. I was able to turn my mess into a powerful message and to God be the glory on that.

Destined for greatness, my journey has broadened my horizons. I completed my Master's in Leadership and now I am pursuing my Doctor of Education degree in Organizational Leadership. I never would have imagined how far I've come, but God positioned me, pushed me, and promoted me to where I am right now. I will always be forever grateful for my 19-year platform of leadership, mistakes, and success in the United States Army and Army Reserves. Hooah!

CHAPTER EIGHT

Medical Diagnosis

Multiple musculoskeletal, neurological, and behavioral health conditions are why my military career is ending. I have been battling a bad back, neck, shoulder, legs, and foot for much of my military career, but I have always sucked it up and kept driving on. This was a mentality carved into my psyche when I began my military career. Pain is just weakness leaving the body, so I sucked it up. I didn't complain or tell anyone, I just drove on. Well, the time for that stinking thinking was over. I had children to care for, a husband to love on, and a life to live beyond the military. I learned to take care of my body because God isn't done with me yet.

God's plan will always supersede your plans and desires. I didn't realize this to be the absolute truth until it happened to me. I planned for one thing and God gave me something else. Once I got that something else I didn't even worry about what I was fighting for. What God gave me was what I was supposed to have.

Years of therapy, referrals, special care, medication, acupuncture, and counseling had now come to a medical board for review. I had exhausted my treatment options and the results were not promising. I have served my country for 19 years and I finally realize that I have more health issues than I wanted to admit. This was a crushing blow to my mind once I finally accepted it. This thinking caused behavioral health conditions that I always told myself I wouldn't get. You never know how you'll feel until you go through it. My husband retired and went through a similar situation and I always wondered why he really felt the way he did. Now I know.

Depression tries to creep in and the thought of no longer being a Soldier has caused mental anguish, depression, and anxiety. The mere thought of me taking off my uniform and replacing it with civilian clothes made me cry. I cried because I had a routine grounded in LDRSHIP - Loyalty, Duty, Respect, Selfless-Service, Honor, Integrity, and Personal Courage, for 19 years and now it was all coming to an end. I cried because I've given my best to thousands of Soldiers, civilians, and government workers on a daily basis and now it is coming to an end.

I never imagined my legs cramping and getting so weak that I couldn't walk through the mall to shop or push a cart through Walmart. I lose my balance and get weak in the knees, my feet hurt constantly and they swell and go numb. My neck and back hurt so bad that I have to take muscle relaxers more often than I ever had to before. I have migraines that cause my vision to get blurry. My left arm has been operated on twice and now I have permanent nerve damage.

Don't allow your promotion, devotion, or job to get so consuming that you forget to take care of you! I wish I would have listened to my body sooner than later, but God has now forced me to pursue my destiny so I have no choice but to follow God's lead. My husband and children need me and I don't want to leave in a body bag. I am now stepping out on faith and allowing God to move me where He wants me to be and to pursue what He wants me to do. I tried this life my way so far, so now Jesus has taken the wheel.

As I look back over my entire life I have always had medical issues but I didn't let them get the best of me because I am still here to talk about it. However, when we neglect ourselves, as I have done multiple times, we eventually have to deal with the aftermath of the neglect and it isn't always pretty. You only get one body and that body you must take of. We often get so wrapped up in life that we care for others and allow other things to consume our souls, that we forget we matter. I had to learn the hard way. God has taken me through this test several times in order for me to finally realize that I must take care of me. I have to remain as healthy as I can for the sake of my children and my legacy building years.

I have now accepted the medical board's decision and I am preparing for my destiny. Nothing happens to us by chance. Everything happens on purpose and there is a divine reasoning behind it. God has a purpose for each of us and the Army was apart of the plan for my life to get me in order, disciplined, aligned, positioned and into proper perspective for where I am about to go next. Every decision, fault, and mistake I made was on purpose to get me to my destiny. I live and breath under the divine covering of Jesus Christ. It is never too late for my body to be healed in order for me to accomplish what the Lord has for me. I know now that my body is precious and it is a temple that must be nurtured, respected, and kept healthy.

CHAPTER NINE

Rear View Mirror

As I look back over my life, I think about all the inappropriate decisions and mistakes I've made, all of the uncalculated risks I've taken, and all of the lies I believed and told. The woman of substance that I have become today is because of it all. I believe everything that happened in my life was on purpose to get me where I am right now. Everything works together for the good, but when you can't see out of your front windshield, you simply turn on your wipers. We can't do that in our real life, we must trust God and walk by faith, not by sight.

In my rearview, I was lonely, depressed, angry, suicidal, anxious, and restless. I was an alcohol dependent, single mother who was consumed with self-doubt while attempting to solve my problems. I'm so glad the rearview mirror is much smaller than my windshield called life. The present and the future has given me the ability to receive God's promises for my life and learn a new way to live with purpose. I have grown so much as a woman and I am glad about it. I could have been dead and gone, locked up in prison, or left at the bottom of the pit. However, the God I serve told me to get up, dust my shoulders off, put my high heels on, and keep walking!

I am glad I don't look like what I've been through. I once doubted myself, called myself names, and threw the towel in, but God said no! I've come a long way, but I still have work to do. Part of that work was to write this book and let you know that it doesn't matter how you start your life, it only matters how you finish. If you feel like you are running out of gas, seek God or a higher being to assist you with life. We think we know it all, but we don't. No one can possibly know everything there is to know about life. Every trial or tribulation I have ever been through was a setup for my greater good. I didn't see it while I was going through my seasons, but now I have a clearer picture of my past. There are somethings I wish I could have changed or never done, but that would have changed the person I am now. Everything was on purpose. Every test, every trial, and every tribulation I had to go through was to see the blessing on the other side. My rearview held all the lessons I needed to be successful as an entrepreneur, leader, speaker, leadership strategist, mother, and wife.

I learned that you must be willing to acknowledge, accept, forgive, and move on from whatever has you bound, hurt, offended, or embarrassed. Stop carrying dead weight and insecurities like a ball and chain on your back and foot.

Let it all go!

That's easier said than done, but try it and God will get you through it. There is nothing too hard for God. I am not telling you anything that I didn't live through myself. I know for a fact that He will work it out because I lived it and learned it.

If you continue to allow your past to assault you, then you will never move forward. Once you acknowledge the issues of your past, figure out how to heal from them by either confronting them head on and forgiving or by giving it to God. Do not carry that energy into your future. Out of the heart, the mouth speaks. A bad heart needs surgery or the words you speak will erupt like a volcano and cut deep like a knife. Be mindful of what you have allowed to grow in your heart. It will lay dormant and fester like a disease. Be willing to heal your heart and love again so you can live your best life. Make better decisions for you. Trust that you will feel so much better.

What's in your rearview mirror? Do you know that everything that happened to you was for a greater purpose? I know it because I no longer look through the rearview mirror because I am confident in who I am. I am confident that my past set me up for my future. I am confident that I am fearfully and wonderfully made. I am confident that my past won't be my legacy, but it set me up for success! I am now able to leave a legacy because of the lessons I've learned from all I have survived. Don't allow your past to define you. If you continue to look in your rearview, you will never go anywhere and you will eventually crash. Look to the hills for whence your help comes from!

CHAPTER TEN

A Lens Of Faith

I am Chaundra Nicole Gore and I am a Lens of Faith. I am a human being, a woman, a mother, and a wife that has gone through hell and back. I have reclaimed my life, wrote my vision, and made it plain. I am stepping out on faith to move by the beat of God's drum for my life. I now have a different perspective on life, a closer relationship with God, and a walk-by-faith mentality like no other. I trust God with my life because He is the Alpha and the Omega, the beginning and the end. He is the author and finisher of my story.

You can see me walk the walk and talk the talk, but I didn't always have it together. I am still learning, but now all the mistakes I made have caused me to be wiser in all my ways. Through prayer and petition, Lens of Faith was birthed to spread the message of now faith. "Now faith is the substance of things hoped for and the evidence of things not seen, (Hebrews 11:1)." I am a walking, living testimony that we are able to conqueror any trial or tribulation that comes our way by having faith in God to see us through. I am a walking testimony to show others that if I can do it, you can, too. LensOfFaith Speaks, LLC was birthed to show the world that there are many souls that are prospering, they have a message to spread and they are living their lives despite the odds against them. Lens Of Faith Photography, LLC was birthed to show the world the image of a beautiful soul through a photographic lens. Each of these businesses was birthed by faith, through faith, and a vision that came to me one day. If I would have never written it down, it probably would never have come to existence.

I am determined to show you better than I can tell you. I asked God to give me the ability to share my story in hopes of blessing another. I birthed Lens of Faith Photography and Lens of Faith Speaks to shine my light onto others, so they can walk in their own light and be who God has called them to be as well. I am a firm believer that God doesn't make mistakes and He gave me the ability, knowledge, and power to be a blessing to others. If I didn't share my truths, then you might not be willing to unpack your pain in order to brighten your tomorrow. We hold on to stuff we are supposed to cast off to God and then we walk around ashamed, hurt, angry, bitter, dead, numb, and psychotic, wondering why. Let it go and live your life to the fullest. Don't allow the chains of your past to show up in your future and block your blessings. Let it go.

In order for me to be a Lens of Faith, I have to download my past and show you my present. I have to show you how I transformed into a success story and how I am unapologetic about it. I stand in my truths in hopes of blessing the masses. What are your truths?

There is glory in your story. I have faith in God to know my pain can be turned into my message. My sexual abuse story can heal someone. My domestic violence story can give someone the guts to leave. The loss of my children can heal someone. The brokenness of my heart can bless someone. The ambushes, waves, and rocks that were in my marriage can touch someone. The bad doctor's reports can give hope to someone. The tribulations I faced with my children can heal someone.

You never know what part of your story will bless another, so tell it and be unapologetic about it! I am a Lens of Faith. I pray this book blessed your life in some way or another. You are now a Lens of Faith, too! God Bless you.

About the Author

Chaundra Nicole Gore is a first time author, leadership strategist, motivational speaker, currently a Master Sergeant in the U.S. Army of 19 Years, Founder and CEO of Lens of Faith Photography LLC, Founder and CEO of LensOfFaith Speaks, a Sexual Assault Victim Advocate, Moderator for Cultivating Clarity in our Community for Domestic Violence, a member Kappa Epsilon Psi Military Sorority Incorporated, an advocate for Service members as a member of The Association for United States Army, Brand Ambassador for We Are Women of Substance, Brand Ambassador for L.I.F.T (Ladies Intentionally Following Through), Brand Ambassador for Black Women Handling Business, a wife, a mother of a blended family, a survivor of domestic violence and sexual abuse.

As a decorated Soldier, Chaundra is a Military award recipient of the Meritorious Service Medal x 3, Army Commendation Medal x 5, Army Achievement Medal x 2, Certificate of Appreciation x 4, Certificate of Excellence x 2 and numerous plaques and coins of excellence for my dedicated service to the United States Army and Army Reserve.

She is married to Kenneth D. Gore Jr. for over ten years and they have a blended family of seven children, Brittany (22), Malik (16), Kamare (14), Makiyah (14), Kenneth III(13), Chloe (9) and Kendrick (5).

Born in Chicago, Chaundra was adopted at the age of 2. Throughout her journey, she has visited various places and has now settled in Lithia, FL. Chaundra has a Bachelor's of Science in Business

Management. A Master's of Science in Leadership. Currently a Doctoral Student at Grand Canyon University. She enjoys shopping for shoes and purses and is an avid book reader. Her favorite quote is, "I Have a Dream," by Dr. Martin Luther King, Jr.

Chaundra's passion is to help heal women who have suffered abuse, anguish, abandonment, suicide, the loss of a child, marriage trouble, career trials and provide resources and tools to help them heal and grow.

She is a rising star who has embraced her faith in God on her journey to her destiny. She has learned more from her losses and failures, than her victories and triumphs. She has embraced change and it all began with her. Change begins with you, if you want to change the results, do something different. Be Bold as A Lion! Just know that faith without work is dead!

www.ingramcontent.com/pod-product-compliance
Lightning Source LLC
Chambersburg PA
CBHW071130090426
42736CB00012B/2077